SAFARI: SNIPPETS OF ADVENTURE

by TOM VOLLERT

ISBN for Paperback: 979-8-9900961-3-4

ISBN for Hardcover: 979-8-9900961-2-7

E book ISBN: 979-8-9900961-1-0

TABLE OF CONTENTS

South Africa 1

The Kitty 3

A Change of Attitude 13

Sundown Visitors 19

A Different Kind of Scenery 23

Silent Wanderers.. 25

A Great Grey Fellow 29

A Precious Family 33

Walking the Bush.. 37

A Great Grey Fellow in the Making........................... 39

Botswana...41

Canids of a Different Kind 43

Teenage Trouble..47

Crowded Canoe Trip 53

Two Interesting Travelers 57

Camp Inspector...61

Didn't Expect To See You There:.............. 65

A Life Survivor.. 69

Nighttime Camp Visitors 72

About the Author... 73

SOUTH AFRICA

Everyone I talked with had the same thought, "Are you nuts going by yourself?" It only took three months to research, plan and make all the arrangements. I did not want to go with a tour group and spend three weeks on an overcrowded tour bus, following other overcrowded tour buses. I wanted to be able to have my own schedule and work on my own projects. A lodge and tent in the middle of the African bush would be perfect. So, that is where I headed off to. Where better to practice my wildlife photography and witness what lures people from around the world to enchanted Africa? I landed at Sabi Sabi Private Game Reserve, located inside Kruger National Park in South Africa. Kruger National Park is 7,523 square miles of African wilderness. The Park is itself a national reserve and the entire Kruger area consists of various private reserves and the national park itself.

After having spent years volunteering in zoos working with exotic animals, from millipedes to gorillas, I was more than ready to immerse myself in what Africa had to offer. And immerse myself I did. Thousands of people travel to Africa every year. Most go to the incredible beaches, shores, and traditional tourist sites. The rest of us head off to find the wildlife. You never know what you will encounter when on safari. Some people spend days seeing very little wildlife and some are lucky enough to see many things and have many experiences. Maybe it's because I subconsciously seek out these experiences, but I am the latter. After boarding three airplanes, touching down at six different landing sites, and about twenty-six hours of airtime I was in a Land Rover and forty-five minutes from my destination.

My bungalow was far from sparse. Spaciously comfortable with a bath, indoor and outdoor shower, sitting room, bedroom, and patio. I would have been happy with a tent and toilet in the ground. Little did I know then that would be my next adventure. Our ranger was Patrick and my traveling companions at Sabi Sabi are two retired couples from New York. Their stay started a couple of days before my stay, and they were scheduled to go home before my trip came to an end. At breakfast on their last day, I learned that one of the gentlemen I had spent the last few days with was once the Prime Minister of Afghanistan. Wow! Look at me! Hob-knobbing with world leaders! There were many people I met from many different countries. Time to get on with finding the wildlife.

THE KITTY

It was my second night, and we were on our second evening game drive. The Land Rovers we use are completely open vehicles. No windows, no doors, no roofs, just seats. My seat of choice was in the very rear, tiered above the seats in front of me. This was a great spot for unobstructed photography. The rangers in each of the vehicles stay connected with one another by radio. This way they can let other guides and ranges know when something of interest is happening. We were alerted this night about a leopard that was close to making a kill, so off we went. When we arrived, she had only moments before brought down a male impala. She had not even started feeding on it yet. There were already three other vehicles at the site, so we pulled up as one end of a semi-circle around the leopard, approximately fifty yards away. There she was, at the base of a large acacia tree lying there with her jaws clamped around the impala's throat.

We sat there watching and waiting for the impala to succumb to the suffocating vise-like grip this leopard had on him. We knew this was a male impala by his horns, we didn't know about the leopard just yet. 10 minutes later the impala struggled for his last breath. In the tall grass this leopard was difficult to see. Even with two or three spotlights on her, she was almost invisible. Her golden yellow coat spotted with solid and rosette style black markings melted her into the landscape perfectly. We would learn in just a little bit of time that she was a large female. Later that week I was to discover she had cubs that had not been far off from her chosen hunting ground that night. Even with four vehicles and

about a dozen and a half people watching her, there was total silence. Everyone's eyes were glued to the scene in the spotlight's glare, watching this magnificent animal at her most primal.

About 20 minutes had passed and our leopard, after opening up her kill, decided to take it into hiding. I thought that she was going to slip past our Land Rovers through the open half of our semi-circle and be off into the bush. The next 10 to 15 minutes would prove that assumption wrong and start an incredible scenario. I, of course, packed down with two cameras, multiple lenses and other gear, had been photographing everything since we arrived, and of course hanging out of the confines of the Land Rover for the best possible angle. The rules, designed for the safety of the animals and the observers, dictate that we do not leave our vehicles. There is relative safety in a vehicle, but when you step out of the vehicle and into the world of wildlife, you are then subject to the rules of nature. And the rules of nature state that you are now eligible to be injured or killed by the true guardians of the bush.

I was hanging out of this vehicle so far and only inches off the ground, that if a grasshopper had landed on my arm, I would have spilled out onto the playing field. With the impala's neck clamped firmly in her jaws and dragging the body between her legs, she started her move towards our vehicle. I was completely immersed in photographing this beautiful animal when I suddenly realized that she was not turning away! She is now only 12 or 15 feet away and I was out of film! Years of working with wildlife have taught me that there are times you just freeze and watch. This becomes an instinct after a while. For the next segment of time, I was frozen where I hang. There are times when you must put the camera down and actually watch what is unfolding in front of you. This was definitely one of those times. You can miss so much

watching only through the lens of a camera. In some way I was glad I had run out of film.

Here she came, getting closer and closer. She was almost close enough to reach out and touch. She was beautiful, tall, and muscular. The impala had to be close to her own weight, if not more, and she was effortlessly dragging him towards us. I could then see the muscles on her in use, pulled taught as she held her head and body upright walking towards us with the impala in her grip. Instinct was kicking in. Do nothing! Be as still and quiet as possible until she walks on by. The only problem with this plan was that she did not walk on by. She stopped directly in front of me! Wow! I wish I had a better word than wow. For someone like me, this just could not get any better. I also knew that this could be an extremely dangerous situation.

This leopard lay down and dropped her kill right in front of me. She looked up directly into my eyes. At this point, she pinned her ears back and started hissing and snarling. I could count every tooth in her mouth. I could smell her breath and feel her saliva on my face as she hissed and spit. I was thinking, yup, those *are* large canines. The blood from the impala covered her cheeks and muzzle. I could not have been more excited! This is the moment that dreams are made of, because at this point, she was only three feet from my face! Let me say this again. She was only three feet from my face. This moment seemed to last forever. She, staring into my eyes and me, staring into her eyes. Her eyes were huge, beautiful, yellow discs, so full of primitive life. If I had thought about it, I could have counted her whiskers she was so close. For a brief time, there was only me, and this leopard. Nothing else existed in the world but the two of us in our own personal drama.

Now what? We had three possible scenarios. 1) She decided to continue back into the bush. 2) She decided I was a threat and attacked me. 3) Well, who knows… she was a wild animal in an incredibly stressful

situation and there were no rules here. I was hoping for number 1, but I also really did want her to stay. Yup, I am nuts.

I knew in the back of my mind that this encounter had to end. Patrick, our ranger, had to move our vehicle. I knew it, but I did not want it to happen. "Patrick, don't you dare move this vehicle" kept playing in my mind. I wanted to play out the entire encounter to the very end. But the safety of the passengers and the animals was Patrick's first priority. So, as I knew he would eventually, Patrick moved the Land Rover. The amazing thing that I want you to think about is this: this leopard at any time could have leapt onto me, seriously injuring, or even killing me. She didn't. For her it was not about killing just because she could, it was about telling me to back off so she could have her dinner in peace. If anything terrible had happened in that encounter, it would have been completely and totally my fault.

After all, it was me that was invading her world uninvited. Over the next few days, I would see this leopard several more times. I felt a connection with her but understood it was my connection and not hers. That was ok with me. When my group next saw her, she was with her cubs. Three little perfect leopards. As my misfortune would have it, I was off hiking in the mountains many miles away and missed seeing the cubs.

Later that evening back at the lodge, I was a bit of a celebrity over dinner. For all the stories that have been witnessed over many years at the lodge, mine was the first encounter with any predator or other dangerous animal, that up close and personal. It was pure chance that the human animal walked away. If my trip had ended then and there, I would have been satisfied with the extra short visit. Days later, I was still wrapped up with the encounter and feeling something, I can't explain, even to this day. My encounter with this leopard I cannot possibly put into words. I think that if I were able to, it would in some way diminish

the entire event. For those few moments, it was only her and me in the entire universe. How can anyone describe that?

Leopards are sleek powerfully built animals. They are capable of bringing down prey more than twice their own weight. They hunt by stealth, and stalk their prey until they are close enough to pounce with a short chase. They have the most widely spread population of all the big cat species. Depending on which scientific text you read there are 28 or 32 types (subspecies) of leopards and are seen in both, the yellow coat with spots or, the black coat with spots.

A Change of Attitude

It was late afternoon, and the shadows were growing longer. Not a lot of daylight left, and we have come across hardly any wildlife except for some impala and birds on the wing overhead. Earlier in the day before we left the lodge, Patrick talked with us about some lions that were thought to have been in the area over the past few days and might be heading in our direction. In vast open places, like where this reserve is situated, "in the area" can be 20 miles away. Knowing this can save you a lot of wasted "getting excited" time anticipating an encounter that will probably never actually occur. Patrick thought that towards the end of our evening drive we would head towards the place the lions might be, if they were actually coming this way. It was time to take a chance and look for the lions, so off we went. Sometimes all the planets in the universe line up at the right time, and magical stuff really does happen. Forty-five minutes after changing direction and driving off-road we were hit with an amazing sight. Lions!! Wow, how did that happen? Does not really matter, we found them and that's all that counts. One, two, three, five….no…seven, seven lions! Three adult females, and four young males. The males were most certainly the offspring of one or more of the females. These young males were beginning to show their manes which put them about 14 to 18 months of age.

There they were, all seven lions lying in a small clearing in the bush. Peacefully lounging about, it seemed as though you could have walked right up and scratched their ears. Definitely, not a good idea!

We watched them for some time, when from off in the distance was the cry of some unknown animal. Bang! instantly all seven lions were standing and looking about, ears perked, eyes burning into the surrounding bush.

It was just incredible how fast they changed, from sleepy lounging lions to extremely alert tracking machines. Then swoosh, they were off. We followed as best we could, but they had melted into the bush and were gone. I was still in awe of the speed of their change in attitude. Sleepy cats to hunting lions. Attempting to track these cats, we had driven through the bush for about 45 minutes, when Patrick stopped the Land Rover, and we began scanning the surrounding area for the lions. I was looking through my lens, panning the bush when bingo... there they were, the four young males.

They were about two hundred yards away sitting on the high, steep bank of a dry riverbed intently staring at something on the opposite bank... our side of the dry riverbed. The bush was much too thick for the Land Rover, and walking would have been extremely danger-ous considering the adult females were still unseen and we could have walked right into them. Not a good idea!

Lions are a top predator in Africa and the largest of the African cats. Females can weigh in at three hundred pounds and males up to five hundred pounds. Contrary to popular belief, lions are responsi-ble for more human deaths in Africa than any other animal. This is particularly true of lions living in parks and reserves that have no fear of humans.

Male lions have a bad and undeserved reputation for being lazy. The truth is, male lions work extremely hard at staying alive. If they have a pride, they must defend it. This means patrolling their territory, hunting their own food, and battling with other male lions who want to take over their pride and territory. These battles can be fierce and

savage, leading to serious wounds and even death. Male lions without a pride must hunt for food and protect themselves from other male lions as they roam the land passing in and out of the territories of other prides – a journey filled with danger. The life expectancy for a male lion is on average, about seven to nine years. That is a rough life by any standard.

Sundown Visitors

It is not every day that a family of warthogs strolls through your dining room in the middle of breakfast, lunch, or dinner. However, here in Africa it is not unusual at all. At the lodges, the wildlife is free to come and go as they please. That is the one reason you never venture out of the lodge area without an armed escort or wander the grounds at night without the company of an armed ranger. If you have learned your lessons from the rangers, you will be able to pick out the lion or leopard tracks that were left the previous night on the lodge grounds. I suppose those tracks I found outside my hut door on a couple of mornings were real! I would check the area in front of my bungalow every morning to see who my overnight visitors were. Of course, the sight of the local baboon troop wandering past your outside shower while you are all lathered up makes for interesting dinner conversation. I wonder what it was they were thinking, as they glanced my way to see this human covered in white lather. It may be a blow to my ego, but I bet they did not even care.

Sundowners are a time during your evening game drives or walks that you stop at sundown or there about and break out drinks and food. It is a tradition dating back to the British colonial times in Africa. Sundowns in Africa are legendary and spectacular. And when the sun finally sets, the night sky is incredible. You can see every star in the sky. When the moon is out the landscape takes on a mysterious aurora and hints as to what was so visible only moments before. Your thinking changes and you start wondering what animals there are in the trees

and bush watching you. On this night, we stopped on an open plane. A perfect full moon, and not a cloud in the sky. Incredible! We opened the rear gate of the Land Rover and set out the food and drinks. The only light was from the moon, and it was more than enough.

Standing at the back of the vehicle talking with Harold, our tracker, I noticed movement out of the corner of my eye. I turned to see what had caught my attention and there were two hyenas not fifteen feet away. As casually as I would talk with anyone, I turned to Harold, and informed him that there were two hyenas standing by the front of the vehicle. Harold acknowledged their presence, and we continued our conversation. They watched us, and we watched them. We continued eating, drinking, and talking. It all seemed so perfectly normal, an everyday occurrence. After a while, the hyenas apparently got bored and left. A little time had passed when we heard a hyena calling off in the distance. It was from the opposite direction our two visitors had disappeared too. Moments later the same two hyenas (I suppose) came trotting past us heading in the direction of the hyena call. It was later back at the lodge when it struck me how comical our encounter really was. Here in the states, you are not likely to have an encounter like that, but to have been so casual about the hyena visit seemed normal. Anything can happen in Africa.

As casual as the hyena visit was, there are some things we need to keep in mind. Hyenas are carnivores. They eat meat. They are large immensely powerful predators. They are not the clumsy scavengers we often hear about. They are very accomplished hunters. In fact, lions scavenge much more food than hyenas are accused of scavenging. Here in Africa hyenas do kill people. There are stories of hyenas pulling people in their sleeping bags as they sleep from around a campfire and dragging them off into the bush. Under a separate set of circumstances or had there possibly been more hyenas in the area, this "casual hyena visit" may have turned out differently and perhaps, tragically.

A Different Kind of Scenery

I had hired a guide, Rob, from one of the local tour/safari out-fits to take me up to the Drakensberg Mountain Range for a day of hiking. South Africa has some spectacular mountain ranges, but the Drakensburg Mountain Range has some incredibly special sites. Our destination was about a three-hour drive, so we started our day at about 6 am. The sun was up early with us, and it was starting to feel warm, so a very mild day in the high country seemed a good possibility. Our first stop was in the Mpumalanga area of the Drakensburg Range. It was not a typical tourist stop and only a couple of vehicles parked nearby.

Rob informed me that he was afraid of heights, and I would be do-ing the hiking solo! Not that I minded, but it would have been nice to have known this earlier. Off I went, beautiful countryside with inter-esting peaks and multiple drop waterfalls. A section of canyon displayed sheer rock walls tinted with a beautiful palette of colors as if they had been painted. The spray from the falls, playing tricks with the color palettes were trance-like, and I think it would have been possible to sit there all day mesmerized.

I continued my hike and stumbled upon a couple on their own hike. I did not expect not to see anyone, but what were the chances of this en-counter? A young couple on holiday, just walking the hills. We stopped and chatted briefly. When I inquired as to where they were from, they said Chicago, IL. Chicago, IL! You must be kidding me! What are the odds of hiking in the mountains of South Africa, with nobody around for miles, in the middle of nowhere and meeting people from Chicago, IL? Speechless!

I eventually made my way back to Rob, without getting lost or falling off the mountain, considering that my guide sent me off on my own, not a bad feat. We next headed to an incredibly famous place known as God's Window that had truly spectacular vistas.

At the overlooks on the mountains there are railings along some of the mountain edge drop offs. And I do mean drop offs, straight down! These railings are minimal and do not prevent you from stepping to the edge. People have fallen off the mountains, looking down over the edges, or have even been blown off by the wind. In some places, there are no railings at all! Several formations on the escarpment resemble precisely, the structure of a quite common African village hut. It makes you wonder if these natural mountain landscapes are the inspiration for dwelling designs of some of the African people.

Blyde River Canyon was next. Here we find the world-famous Bourke's Luck Potholes, named after British gold miner Tom Bourke. The potholes are natural occurrences where whirlpools of water have cut perfectly smooth, round, spiral looking holes into the bedrock. The canyon is littered with them. The canyon walls have been carved extremely smooth by the water entering the canyon. The potholes range in width from a few feet to a few yards. I cannot describe these places and sights to do them justice. They must be viewed to be genuinely appreciated.

Silent Wanderers

Often in the bush you will be just yards away from an animal and never know it. It is entirely possible to walk up onto a pride of lions sitting on a kill, or a cape buffalo behind a stand of trees and never see them until you're right on top of them. These can be extremely dangerous encounters. Anything is possible in Africa. It is important to understand your surroundings. It could mean the difference between flying home in the passenger section or in a box in the cargo hold. Animals are so well adapted to blending into their surroundings, it is magical. Most of the time, it is oh so quiet in the bush. You can be in the middle of a herd of cape buffalo consisting of two hundred or more animals and hear nothing except the sound of chewing as they walk right by. After they have passed, it is silent again, but for the birds and insects stirred up in their wake. Amazing! Having done that several times I can tell you it is completely true.

Patrick knew of a large herd of cape buffalo and where they were heading too. Patrick parked the Land Rover one hundred yards away from them, directly in their path. Not long after, we were in their midst, and they were calm and content. It was possible to reach out and touch them. Not a good idea! They flowed by and disappeared into the bush in almost total silence. How can that be? Sitting amid three hundred plus animals, weighing an average of fifteen hundred pounds, and walking past you in almost total silence is spectacular. This herd consisted of adult females, calves, sub-adult males and females and a few young adult males. Typically, the old crotchety bulls spend their time away

from the herds in bachelor groups. You really do not want to mess with these animals. Cape buffalo are extremely dangerous animals. They are responsible for many injuries and deaths in Africa. They are typically very ill-tempered when disturbed and older bulls take no guff from anyone or anything. They are spectacular when defending their young and members of the herd, often injuring, even killing predators such as lions and hyenas. When coming to the rescue of a herd member in distress they may charge en masse, driving off the predators.

A GREAT GREY FELLOW

The four other people in my safari group did not participate in the daily bush walks. This was an excellent opportunity for Patrick and me to spend extended time in the bush. Walking through the bush with an exceptionally knowledgeable ranger like Patrick is like taking college classes in the wild. Even the things you learn that have nothing to do with wildlife are amazing. On this afternoon, we were following lion tracks along a dirt road when we came around a curve in the road and were greeted with the sight of a handsome bull elephant browsing on some acacia tree branches. He was only 30 or 40 yards away.

Because Patrick and I were always quiet on our walks, this elephant did not realize we were right behind him. We froze where we were and kneeled one leg to the ground. The important thing here was to remain quiet and not disturb this giant. If sufficiently provoked or surprised, this giant grey powerhouse could easily turn our day into an awfully bad dream. It was about 10 or 15 minutes later when the wind changed, and our giant grey friend realized he had company. At first, he stopped eating and turned our way for a look see. After shaking his head and flapping his ears at us, he went back to eating. Patrick thought it would be ok for us to move and get a better viewing angle if we kept our distance since he now knew we were there. Unfortunately, our big grey friend did not like being left out of the decision-making process and when we started our move abruptly halted lunch, whirled around in our direction, threw his ears forward again, bellowed and took two very impressive steps towards us.

Patrick and I held our ground and tried not to appear threatening by making any sudden moves like running, which might provoke a charge. After making his point, he went back to eating. Another minute or two went by and our elephant friend again made us aware of his displeasure with us by whirling around, shaking his head, bellowing, flapping his ears, and taking another two very impressive steps towards us. Ok, time to go! I can take a hint. If a lion charges, you stand your ground. If an elephant even hints at charging you, you go. Slowly we backed off into the bush until we were out of sight, checking over our shoulders along the way, making sure we were not being followed by our unhappy grey friend. If that elephant had charged, there was no conceivable way we could have outrun him.

Elephants are amazingly fast. As fast as 30 mph will take you. While we would be running through the bush dodging trees and bushes, that elephant would be mowing them down like twigs and be on top of us in no time. Most times an elephant's charge is all bluff, but you may never really know until it is too late. An African bull elephant can stand thirteen feet tall and weighs in at 12 to 13 tones. His tusks can weigh in at over two hundred pounds each and reach a length of ten feet or more. An elephant's tusk is a modified tooth that can last a lifetime or be broken off from being used as a lever or having been in battle with another bull.

Quite an intimidating presence! Now what kind of photographer would I have been if I had not taken any photographs throughout that whole encounter? There was not time for many, but I managed a few. I am only glad I did not have to ditch my equipment while trying to run through the bush.

A Precious Family

The Land Rover turned back onto the dirt road and the dust started whipping about. Always trying to be vigilant and aware of my surroundings, I am always looking around to see what's going on behind and to the sides of us. Turning to look back at the trail we just left I made a discovery. Hippos! I yelled to Patrick, and he yelled back, what?? I knew immediately what he meant. Hippos generally are not running around in the bush miles away from water. In my excitement, I yelled hippos when I meant rhinos. Vollert, you idiot, I was thinking. I corrected myself and Patrick swung the Land Rover around. A mother white rhino and her young calf had crossed the trail behind us. If I had not been watching, we never would have seen them and would have missed something incredibly special. We followed them a short distance down the road to a large open field. Mom and her calf stopped here to graze.

Mom was beautiful. She was huge and displayed an incredible four foot long, perfectly formed, and curved front horn. Her calf was tiny, compared to her enormous size, incredibly cute and about four to five weeks old. This was not an easy photo shoot. Mom was very protective of her calf, and the calf was very shy. Mom continually placed herself between her calf and us, and when the rare opportunity to see her calf surfaced, the baby turned and ran off. It was great just to watch them, even without getting the photos I wanted.

This was a rare opportunity and the few photos I managed to take will help keep this memory alive. Rhinos appear in two different

versions in Africa. The white rhino, and the black rhino. The white rhino is larger and feeds as a grazer. The black rhino is a browser and typically has a grumpier disposition. Both animals have poor eyesight and can be extremely dangerous when threatened. The term white in the name white rhinoceros is a mistranslation of the Dutch word "wide", referring to the shape of the animal's mouth. The origin of the black rhino's name is not known for sure but thought to have been derived as a distinction from the white rhino's name and from the dark colored soil that often covers the black rhino.

WALKING THE BUSH

The best way to walk the bush is to imitate the wildlife. Walking the bush can be dangerous and there are numerous ways to get yourself into trouble. You need to pay attention to your surroundings. Stay on the trail, walk in single file, and stop, look, and listen. Patrick and I had taken numerous walks in the bush and never really got into any trouble. Walking the trail makes your walk less tedious. You are walking on ground that has been worn into a pre-made path and you do not have to stumble over rocks, bushes, and holes. If you were to come upon a venomous snake, it is more likely that only one member of your group is going to be bitten.

Okay, I know, nobody wants to get bitten, but survival in the bush for man and animal means reducing the risk of injury. Patrick and I had just such an encounter when a black mamba, probably the most feared venomous snake in Africa, raced across our trail less than a foot in front of Patrick. Black mambas can grow to a length of fourteen feet, are slightly built snakes unlike the heavy body of a python. They are known to be extremely aggressive to the point of chasing people down. The average speed of most snakes is around eight miles per hour, black mambas can manage an impressive 10 to 12 mph. Now granted, the snake we encountered was just a youngster only a about 2 ½ feet in length, but it could have been twelve feet in length. Keep in mind that the bite of a 2-foot mamba can be just as deadly as that of a large mamba.

We stop, look, and listen when walking the bush so that we know what is happening around us. We do this frequently. Being vigilant of our surroundings helps us to avoid walking into trouble and keeps us aware of what is happening around us. Walking can dull the senses, as your mind tends to wander and being unaware can be dangerous. The wildlife have been navigating the bush for thousands of years and have gotten it down pretty well. Why change something that works? Walking the bush is an exciting experience whether it is your first or hundredth time.

I'm sure there are those who would disagree, but you'll never convince me otherwise.

A Great Grey Fellow in the Making

We were skirting the tree line in our Land Rover when we noticed a small breeding herd of elephants heading toward the open plane. Patrick headed toward their track and parked us nearby. They were walking mostly single file and heading towards our parking spot. One of the youngsters, about 1 year old, decided to show us how brave and intimidating he was. With tree branch in hand, or mouth in this case, ears spread out to show us his enormous size, he charged our vehicle in his best imitation of a giant bull elephant. His mother and the rest of his family carried on and paid us no attention. After a few moments of staring us down, he spun off back to his mom. This was very comical, and we tried not to laugh too hard so as not to embarrass him too much. After all, in a few years down the road when he is thirteen feet tall and weighs 14 tons, he may come looking for the tiny humans that embarrassed him that day. Still considered a calf at this age, he has another 13 to 15 years before he leaves his family and start his adult life with other male elephants. When young adult males are pushed out of their family herds they may hang around on the outskirts of the herd until they finally wander off in search of other adult males. Adult males generally live in loosely formed bachelor groups, returning to the breading herds for mating.

BOTSWANA

Another adventure brings me to Botswana. The Central Kalahari
Game Reserve, Chobe National Park, Moremi Game Reserve, and The
Okavango Delta. These were our camping destinations. Each of these
parks has a vastly different landscape and are all spectacular in their
own way. Mobile tenting camping, hot showers under a bucket of water
heated over a fire and holes in the ground toilets. Perfect! If that's not
luxury camping, then what is? My traveling companions are two couples from England and a woman from Australia. Our camps consisted
of four tents in a semicircle for guests and tents and equipment for the
camp staff off to the side. My tent was at the end of our semicircle.
The first night brings sounds of the surrounding forest crashing down
around you. Total darkness, nothing to see. Only the sounds of wood
being splintered and torn apart. A walk around the camp in the early
morning light brings into view what all the night's commotion was
about. Trees torn apart, branches and debris all over the ground. There
is only one answer for this. Elephants! A small group of elephants had
visited camp during the night for a late-night snack. It had been either
a bachelor group or a breeding herd and nowhere to be seen now. The
animals themselves had been ghostly quiet. Only the noise of the trees
being torn apart was evidence of their presence. Some of these awesome
critters were only feet from some of the tents, and still, the animals were
silent. This would not be the same scenario on our last night in camp.

The plan for this adventure was mobile camping. Every three to
four days we would break camp and head to another park or area of

a park. Sometimes the drive was several hours and other times only a couple of hours. The advantage of driving to these different campsites was that we could still have awesome wildlife viewing along the way.

One late afternoon we sat for about two hours at a hyena den watching the youngsters romp and play. These little guys were about five months old and having a grand old time. Typically, it is the matriarch of the clan that produces litters. The female pups in the litter are the dominant pups as is their mother with the adults. The females dominate hyena clans. Female pups will dominate their brothers, sometimes to the extent of ending a brothers' life. A dominant female pup may even kill a less dominant sister. This pup typically inherits the matriarchal position when her mothers' life ends, or outright takes it from her mother. These pups are serious from the start of their lives.

Canids of a Different Kind

African wild dogs, also known as painted wolves, are one of the most sought-after animals to see. African wild dogs as it turns out, are neither dogs nor wolves but are in the Canidae family. These animals are tall, sleek, with coats painted with the most amazing, mottled caramel brown and white colors, with giant ears that are way too big for their heads, giving them a very distinctive look. One of our game drives was planned specifically to find these awesome animals. CD knew exactly where to find the local pack. They were in a clearing on the edge of the bushveld frolicking like a school yard full of children. The pack looked to be about 20 – 25 animals consisting of adults, sub-adults, and pups. The pups, chasing each other, playing keep away with whatever they could grab with their mouths with the occasional wrestling match were magical to watch. An incredible sight!

It was late in the day and time for dinner. Time for this pack to hunt. The pups were old enough to accompany the rest of the pack during a hunt so off the whole group went. If the pups had not been old enough to go on this hunt, they would have stayed at the den with one or more babysitters to watch over them. The dogs started off by trotting through the bush sniffing the air and ground hoping to find a scent that would lead them to a quarry. Although the pups are old enough to tag along on the hunt, they are still playful and not as focused as the adults. CD thought it would be a good time for the dogs to show us a very interesting behavior. CD called out, mimicking a distress call the dogs would make if one or more of the pack members were in trouble.

Instantly all the dogs, including the pups, stopped in their tracks, perking up their ears and sniffing the air.

Every dog in the pack was on high alert, looking around trying to locate where this pack member was calling from. CD made no other vocalizations, so the pack had no other information to act on but still spent time trying to determine if there was a pack member in trouble. We sat with them for nearly half an hour before they decided to return to their original plan. It was amazing to have seen how these dogs reacted to a potential pack member in trouble. No questions asked. Instant loyalty to protect pack members.

TEENAGE TROUBLE

On our drive back to camp we came upon a bit of a roadblock. Another vehicle ahead of us had stopped at a small river crossing where several elephant bulls were hanging around. There were two large older bulls taking advantage of a small pond just off the river to our left. You knew they were older wiser bulls by their demeanor, just hanging out, not paying much attention to the three younger teenagers making a ruckus. It seemed that the driver ahead of us was hesitant to cross the river because of the antics of the youngsters. As we waited for this driver to decide what to do it started turning dark, and quickly. Elephants at night are very wary of unusual noises and flashing lights. A skittish frightened elephant is no joke and an animal to be avoided at all costs. You have probably figured out why I am setting up this story. Yup! The clueless driver in front of us decided to rev his engine, blare his horn, and flash his lights to warn off the youngsters. Not his best decision. The three youngsters panicked! Off into the woods they ran screaming, trumpeting, and trashing the vegetation around them. The driver ahead of us made his getaway.

We were up next. Our ranger, CD, waited a bit to see what the youngsters were going to do. They had not yet returned from the woods, so we started across the river. At that moment one of the youngsters came barreling out of the woods at us from behind. Screaming and trumpeting he bored after us like a freight train. A half second later another youngster came at us from our right, also screaming and trumpeting. I yelled at CD, "He's coming, he's coming! This youngster was

less than 10 yards from the Land Rover. I was sure we were going to get smacked! CD was calm and focused. He pushed the accelerator pedal through the floor and off we went with both juveniles chasing us for the next 20 or 30 yards. With all this commotion going on, the two old bulls in the pond continued to eat and bathe. Not a care in the world! What a splendid example of older and wiser. The three other safari travelers in our group were both excited and shaken. It was a little while before we could no longer hear the juveniles making their ruckus. With smiles and expressions of awe we talked about the adventure for the rest of the evening. The next morning at breakfast our nighttime adventure was the first topic of the day.

I have always been excellent at spotting wildlife. I am not bragging. It just comes naturally to me. Whether driving down an interstate or traveling through the bushveld, wildlife just pops into view for me, even if I am not actively looking. There are times when my fellow travelers do not believe what I'm seeing until either it moves or walks into view. I have had rangers and guides ask me to be their spotter on safari trips. One time when this skill came into play, we were trying to locate a lion we had lost sight of. He had walked into the deep bushveld and vanished. CD, using his keen knowledge and years of experience decided on the direction we should go to try and spot our handsome friend. This lion was one half of a duo that had an incredible story that we will get to further on in our story.

As we drove along the rutted dirt track, I was scanning the bush with both my eyes and my camera lens. I spotted a shape a couple of hundred yards into the bush in a small clearing. It was like a window to a specific spot. I yelled to CD that I thought I had found our friend and asked him to back up to the window in the bush. A quick glance into my camera confirmed what I thought I had found. Our fully maned handsome friend was lying down in a tiny clearing. When I

am searching for wildlife, I look for shapes that are not random, shapes that do not seem to be part of the general area, and shapes that seem to move. Our friend was posed in a typical side view of a lion lying prone and half sitting up. That is what caught my eye. A shape that should not have been there. CD recognized him almost immediately and our companions, after having some initial trouble finding him, and with some directional guidance finally found our friend. He was so far off he was mostly just a shape. Too far for photos. He eventually moved off and that was the last we saw of him, but not our last interaction.

CROWDED CANOE TRIP

We were looking forward to a picnic on the shores of one of the tributaries in the Okavango Delta area. We were to take a canoe trip, explore the delta and park along the way for a picnic lunch. Our guides for this trip gave an outline of our itinerary and a safety talk. They reminded us of the presence of hippos in the delta. Hippos like deeper water than what the tributaries were currently at, and they were confident that we wouldn't need to worry about the hippos but to stay alert – as everyone should, no matter where you were when out in the wild. It was a great day for a canoe trip, bright blue skies with a very soft cloud cover here and there. Not ten minutes into our trip the world changed. Two hippos that prefer deeper water decided this day that they were interested in not so deep water. This is the type of adventure that follows me around.

As we turned the bend, we came face to face with a hippo. This hippo was probably a hundred yards ahead of us just staring us down. He, or she heard us coming and was ready and waiting. We came to a stop. With no place to get off the water our guides started to back us up very slowly. Moments later we heard a very large splash. To our rear a second hippo entered the water, and we stopped once again. This hippo was closer but not making any effort towards us. The hippo to our front was also content to stay put. The water was not deep enough for them to submerge. With the water coming only to the underside of their abdomen they looked gigantic just standing there. We sat there for ten to twelve minutes, although it seemed longer, our guides telling us to stay still, quiet and calm. Our group was in three canoes, now

53

next to each other, bobbing in the tiny waves generated by the current. Suddenly both hippos started vocalizing, splashed through the water into the vegetation that blankets the shores and disappeared into the tall grass. We stayed put for the next ten to fifteen minutes waiting to see if these two hippos would come back. They did not and our guides decided we would be safer heading back to our launching beach. Hippos are extremely territorial and extremely dangerous when they perceive a threat. Hippos are responsible for a large number of human deaths in Africa every year. Male hippos can weigh as much as nine-thousand pounds, females may reach three thousand pounds, with canine teeth reaching lengths of twenty inches.

In all my trips to Africa, and of all my little adventures, this was the first time I was worried about the outcome of an interaction with wild-life. If either one of these hippos, or both, had decided to come at us, I didn't have a plan to escape the danger. We would have been completely at their mercy.

Two Interesting Travelers

Word was circulating between the local people and the rangers working in the area that two adult male lions had recently arrived in the area. These lions had never been seen before and it was a mystery regarding where they come from. These two lions were causing quite a stir with the resident lion pride, and we had seen some of the chaos. One night these lions had stolen a cape buffalo kill from the resident pride. Campers in the area had heard the terrible sounds of lions fighting. On the following day we came across a young male lion and an adult female from this pride. They were lying under a large acacia tree and looking very beat up. The male was licking his wounds and the female was lying prone nearby. Both animals were covered in blood.

Lions are incredibly tough and resilient animals and although these two were very beat up they seemed to be not seriously hurt. Later in the day we stumbled across the cape buffalo kill the resident pride had made the night before. It was abandoned. How could this be possible? Most of the buffalo was untouched. This was very strange and unusual. We would have expected to see the kill mostly consumed… lions, hyenas, or vultures feasting on the remains or at least nearby. There were not even vulture droppings on the buffalo and no other animals nearby. After the two new intruders had driven off the resident pride no other animals had come to claim the buffalo. Insects were the only caretakers of this buffalo now.

The following day we spotted the two intruders. We knew they were two troublemakers by their appearance. Besides being exceptionally

large, fully maned adult lions, they were very dark in color. The resi-dent lions, and other lions in the area were much lighter in color. Their appearance was very intimidating. They looked like they were ready to take on the world! We followed them for about a mile when they split up. We lost sight of one, but we were able to follow the other until he walked off into the deep bushveld and vanished. Over the next few days, we heard these two formidable lions roaring in the middle of the night. Lion roars can be heard for several miles, so it can be hard to know where they are. The rangers surmised that these two intruders had put such fear in to the local wildlife that no animal dared go near the buffalo kill. We drove by this buffalo several times over the next couple of days and the buffalo was still untouched. Finally, after four days the local vulture population could wait no longer and took own-ership of the buffalo kill.

Camp Inspector

We arrived at our new campsite in the late afternoon. When one heads off to new areas to explore, the camp staff breaks down the camp, heads to the new location and sets up camp all over again. These were very busy days for them and a lot of work. When we got to the new campsite it was as if we'd never left the first camp. All our tents were completely set up and ready for guests. This included each tent shower, the toilets that needed to be dug out, cots, tables, and washing stations. Then there were the common areas that also needed to be set up as well, the kitchen and dining area, and the camp staff tents and amenities. These staff members do an awesome job and are always ready with a smile and offers to help if needed.

Typically, after a day of driving and exploring we came back to camp for a shower, wind-down time and dinner. The shower and toilet area behind each tent was a squared off area draped with canvas walls. While in the middle of my shower this day, I noticed a large grey form looming above the canvas walls moving toward camp. A peek over the wall confirmed the large grey form to be a bull elephant. I quickly finished my shower, dressed, and headed out of the tent. I watched as this giant casually strolled into camp as though he were joining our group. I yelled out "elephant in the camp" to let the rest of my group know we had company. This elephant was so relaxed and casual it was comical. He explored the vehicles with his trunk, sniffed out the fire pit, and inspected a couple of tents. The rest of my group stayed in their tents and watched from their doorways as the camp staff watched from their

workstations. He stayed with us for about fifteen minutes, exploring the camp, and munching some foliage. When he was satisfied that everything was proper, he made his way out of camp and wandered off back to the bush. The camp sites we used are sites that are used by several of the tour companies on a regular basis. At dinner, CD let us know that this particular elephant makes it a habit of visiting campsites along his travel route. This was a very comical story and certainly a very unexpected visit from the locals.

DIDN'T EXPECT TO SEE YOU THERE:

After a dusty morning drive, we stopped for lunch. We parked near the bank of a large pond under the branches of a very large acacia tree. Several hundred yards past the far shore of the pond was a sight not often seen. To say we were looking at a large herd of cape buffalo would be the world's biggest understatement. This herd filled our view from left to right as they slowly strolled along while grazing. CD estimated the herd size at somewhere near 2500 animals. It was nearly a half hour before they were out of sight. A very humbling experience. With a little free time, I decided to wander around a bit, not straying too far from the Land Rover. Remember, there were animals there more than willing to wreck your day. I turned the corner onto a well-used track just off the clearing where we stopped for lunch, scanning the trees and ground for something interesting. When I looked up a got a little bit of a surprise. About fifty or sixty yards ahead of me was a lone, adult, male, cape buffalo. Coming to an instant stop I started planning out the next few minutes of possible scenarios in my mind before they happened or didn't happen. One of the lessons I have learned is to have a plan for the unexpected. Although this incredible looking animal was a little ways off, he could still be on top of me before I got very far if I needed to run. I started making a mental note of climbable trees and hiding places nearby. The buffalo and I watched each other for a while. At the same moment we both decided to walk away. He wasn't much worried about me as he snorted, shook his huge head, turned, and trotted away. I, on the other hand, was keenly aware of what this awesome animal was capable of and walked away backwards, keeping an eye on my new best friend.

A Life Survivor

We were sitting at a man-made watering hole. Man-made watering holes are a common sight in the wildlife parks. They supply lifesaving water to the resident and transient wildlife roaming the countryside. Sometimes they are cement block structures in the shape of giant troughs or just dugout holes in the ground. We were watching about twenty bull elephants hanging around this dugout watering hole, some drinking and others just interacting with each other. They were all very relaxed without a care in the world. I noticed in the distance a lone cape buffalo trotting in our direction. As he came into view, I could see he was a warrior and survivor of many encounters. He had one broken horn, both ears were ragged and torn, his right ear appeared to have had a quarter of it bitten off. He had a very large hole in his right side and large scars and scrapes over many areas of his body. His facial expression was that of an old, tired warrior that was not yet ready to give up. Two ox peckers were riding his shoulders picking off parasites on his skin. He had a bad limp in his right rear leg. But here he was trotting along at a very quick pace.

His destination was the watering hole. His next problem was how to get through all those bull elephants blocking the watering hole. This buffalo was an amazing creature. He poked around looking for a break in the wall of elephant bodies, one side of the group to the other side of the group, none of the elephants giving way. Finally, he found a gap. He wedged his way between some very large bodies and wham! Suddenly, the group of elephants noticed his presence in their midst, and they all

bolted out of and away from the waterhole. This impressive buffalo now had the entire waterhole to himself! He slowly lowered himself into the cooling water, wiggled for a comfortable spot and just relaxed his whole body in the water.

I asked myself how this animal could still be alive. He'd obviously had some battles and had survived them all. I could not believe that he had not become dinner for a pride of lions or a hyena clan somewhere in the past. All the animals I have photographed have a life story. Some stories are more interesting than others, but all have a tale to tell. What was the life story of this buffalo? It must be incredible. I will never know. I can only imagine what he has experienced.

NIGHTTIME CAMP VISITORS

The night of our next to last day in Botswana we had a great dinner prepared by the camp staff. We talked about where we had visited, the great experiences we'd had and the impressive sights and interactions we had witnessed. CD was always with us for breakfasts, dinners, and nights around the campfires. It was getting late and time to call it a night. Somewhere later in the evening after the camp was asleep, two noisy visitors awakened us. Our two intruders were in camp and were roaring all they could. It was total darkness. You could not see anything ten feet in front of you. We knew they were in camp because this time the roaring worked its way right through you! There is no way to explain the feeling of a lion's roar as it resonates in all your being. This was both very impressive and a little unnerving. There was no way to tell exactly where they were, and knowing how menacing these two lions were, what if they decided to investigate one or more of the tents – this time our camp was in a national area of the park and that means no firearms. No one including the rangers and camp staff had firearms. Let us think about that for a minute. For myself, I knew in the back of my mind all the things that could go wrong here, but I was concentrating on the lions and hoping for a glimpse. Yup, I am nuts! An hour later they were gone. Leaving as silently as they came.

The stories I have written about are just a hint of adventures that can be experienced when visiting Africa. Some of these animals I have encountered will be with me forever. Their lives and experiences are unmatched to anything I will ever experience. The admiration and respect I have for these impressive animals is more than I can describe.

ABOUT THE AUTHOR TOM VOLLERT

Tom Vollert has been a wildlife enthusiast since childhood. Born in California and moving to Massachusetts as a toddler, Tom spent many a lazy day as a young boy, following the local wildlife through the woods and waterways of his suburban Boston Massachusetts home. Playing sports, acting in theatre productions, and volunteering in zoos as an educator, researcher, and animal keeper occupied his free time throughout his adult life. Tom found his love for wildlife photography later in life and was a print and photographic contributor for Africa and Beyond Magazine. He has worked as a design engineer and has been working in veterinary hospitals as an administrator for over 20 years. Wildlife conservation and wildlife rights are a major focus for Tom.

b89c336d-ae23-483b-ad49-e5b17e716b0fR02